LOOK, LOOK AGAIN

A PICTURE PUZZLE CHALLENGE

by Matt Bruning

Capstone
press

HOW TO PLAY:

Look at the photo pair below. Now, look again!
Can you spot the difference?

Do you see it? That's right! The hat color changed from red to blue.

Master the photo puzzles in this book in two easy steps:
    1. Study the photo on the left.
    2. Look at the photo on the right to spot the differences.

More Puzzle Fun:
    • Challenge a friend to see who can solve the most puzzles.
    • See how long it takes you and a friend to solve the
      same puzzle. Whoever solves the puzzle first wins!

Table of Contents

easy

six simple differences

PENGUIN PALS

Spot **6** differences while these
penguin chicks snuggle for warmth.

You're on the right track! But can you spot **6** differences in this photo?

GOOFY GRIN

Find **6** changes before this cheetah stops smiling.

BURNING RUBBER

Start your engines! Spot 6 differences to race through this picture puzzle.

BABY BILLY GOAT

No kidding around! There are **6** differences hidden in this photo.

DIRT DIGGER

Dig up all  changes buried in this photo.

PRANCING PEACOCK

Can you pick out **6** differences while the peacock shows off his feathers?

POWDER PRO

Spot 6 differences in this snowy photo.

HAPPY HIPPOS

Can you find **6** changes before this mother
and calf finish their drink?

MEGA CHOPPER

Try to find **6** differences hovering in this picture puzzle.

GENTLE GIRAFFE

Say cheese! Spot **6** changes before you move
to the next picture puzzle.

TEE-OFF TIME

Fore! You'll need to spot **6** differences
to shoot par in this puzzle.

answer key

page 7

page 9

page 11

page 13

answer key

page 15

page 17

page 19

page 21

page 23

page 25

page 27

page 29

SMALL SPOTS

Look up! Look down! Do you see **8** changes hidden in this photo?

FLAME BUSTER

Things are heating up! Can you
spot 8 hidden changes?

DANCING DOLPHINS

Sploosh! Spot **8** differences while these dolphins play.

See if you can find **8** differences
before the skater finishes his trick.

TINY TRUNKS

Spot **8** differences hidden in this elephant herd.

SPEED SHREDDER

Help these farmers harvest their field.
Find 8 differences as quickly as you can.

FUNNY FISH

**Think you're pretty good? Not so fast.
Try to find all 8 fishy changes.**

Spot 8 changes while these players shoot hoops.

SLEEPY FAWN

**Don't snooze your way through this puzzle.
Stay awake to find all 8 differences.**

GREAT APES

Look closely to spot **8** differences
while these gorillas take it easy.

WIND RIDERS

Can you spot **8** differences before these kite surfers blow away?

answer key

page 37

page 39

page 41

page 43

answer key

page 45

page 47

page 49

page 51

page 53

page 55

page 57

page 59

hard

ten advanced alterations

Dive right into this puzzle and spot
10 differences floating around.

FLAMINGO PARTY

Birds of a feather flock together. Find **10** changes in this picture puzzle.

Try to tackle the 10 differences
hidden in this football photo.

LITTLE CHICKS

Can you spot **10** changes nesting with these baby chicks?

EARTH MOVER

This puzzle could get a little rocky. Try to find 10 differences in this photo.

MONKEY MOUNTAIN

These baboons are hiding **10** changes.
Can you spot them all?

Wow! You're getting good at this. Let's see if you can find **10** differences here. Don't strike out!

ROWDY RACCOON

Hang on! You're not done yet. Spot **10** differences in this picture puzzle.

STEEL BIRD

You're flying through these puzzles.
But can you find all **10** differences?

Spot **10** changes while these deer stop to rest.

Giddyap! Find **10** differences
before you jump to the next puzzle.

answer key

page 67

page 69

page 71

page 73

FUZZY FELINE

Meow! Spot **12** differences while this kitten snoops around.

Can you spot **12** changes
stacked up in this photo?

BRIGHT BIRDS

Find **12** differences before these parrots fly away.

TRACK KINGS

**Think you're an expert? Not so fast.
Pick up the pace to find all 12 changes.**

BIRDIE BREAKFAST

Tweet, tweet! Find **12** hidden changes before these birds finish their food.

ELEPHANT TRAIN

All aboard! Spot **12** differences while these zebras wait for the next train.

Go team! Spot **12** differences while the goalkeeper tries to catch the ball.

STRIPE TIME

These zany zebras are hiding **12** changes.
Can you find them all?

CITY BUILDER

Spot **12** changes hidden in the city.

WILD WHALES

Spot **12** differences while these whales wow the crowd.

DIRT BIKERS

This is it! Prove you're a pro, and find these last **12** differences.

answer key

page 97

page 99

page 101

page 103

answer key

page 105

page 107

page 109

page 111

page 113

page 115

page 117

page 119

index

Published by Capstone Press,
151 Good Counsel Drive, P.O. Box 669, Mankato, Minnesota 56002.
www.capstonepress.com

Books published by Capstone Press are manufactured with paper
containing at least 10 percent post-consumer waste.

Library of Congress Cataloging-in-Publication Data
Bruning, Matt.
    Look, look again : a picture puzzle challenge / by Matt Bruning.
      p. cm.
    Summary: "Simple text invites readers to spot the differences in animal-themed,
machine-themed, and sports-themed picture puzzles" — Provided by publisher.
    ISBN 978-1-4296-4253-8 (softcover)
    1. Picture puzzles — Juvenile literature. I. Title.
GV1507.P47B778 2010
793.73 — dc22   2009024425

042010
005684R

Credits

Megan Peterson, editor; Matt Bruning, designer; Wanda Winch, media researcher

Photo Credits

Digital Vision (Getty Images), 6, 7, 8, 9, 31 (top left, top right), 104, 105, 122 (top left); Photodisc, 82, 83, 93 (top left); Shutterstock/Abrahams, 36, 37, 61 (top left); Shutterstock/Aleksandr Frolov, 78, 79, 92 (bottom left); Shutterstock /Anyka, 96, 97, 121 (top left); Shutterstock/Artur Bogacki, 24, 25, 33 (top right); Shutterstock/beltsazar, 56, 57, 63 (bottom left); Shutterstock/Brent Walker, 70, 71, 91 (bottom left); Shutterstock/Christian Lagerek, 98, 99, 121 (top right); Shutterstock/Christina Richards, 38, 39, 61 (top right); Shutterstock/Dennis Donohue, 22, 23, 33 (top left); Shutterstock/El-dad Yitzhak, 86, 87, 93 (bottom left); Shutterstock/Geoffrey Whiting, 112, 113, 123 (top left); Shutterstock/Gilles Lougassi, 16, 17, 32 (top right); Shutterstock/Glenda M. Powers, 26, 27, 33 (bottom left); Shutterstock/Harald Hoiland Tjostheim, 68, 69, 91 (top right); Shutterstock/Herbert Kratky, 72, 73, 91 (bottom right); Shutterstock/Inc, 58, 59, 63 (bottom right); Shutterstock/Jeff R. Clow, 42, 43, 61 (bottom right); Shutterstock/John Carnemolla, 44, 45, 62 (top left); Shutterstock/Jonathan Larsen, 102, 103, 110, 111, 121 (bottom right), 122 (bottom right); Shutterstock/Joy Brown, 66, 67, 91 (top left); Shutterstock/Junker, 2, 28, 29, 33 (bottom right); Shutterstock/Juriah Mosin, cover (all), 1(all), 100, 101, 121 (bottom left); Shutterstock/Karel Bro , 52, 53, 63 (top left); Shutterstock/KPegg, 80, 81, 92 (bottom right); Shutterstock/Lee Prince, 76, 77, 92 (top right); Shutterstock/Leonid Shcheglov, 46, 47, 62 (top right); Shutterstock/Lucian Coman, 84, 85, 93 (top right); Shutterstock/Maki Ridenour, 116, 117, 123 (bottom left); Shutterstock/Marfot, 9, 17, 24, 39, 47, 55, 69, 77, 84, 99, 107, 114 (tire track all); Shutterstock/Mayskyphoto, 50, 51, 62 (bottom right); Shutterstock/Michael Jung, 40, 41, 61 (bottom left); Shutterstock/Michael Stokes, 54, 55, 63 (top right); Shutterstock/mmm, 114, 115, 123 (top right); Shutterstock/Morgan Lane Photography, 21 (snowman); Shutterstock/Neale Cousland, 18, 19, 32 (bottom left); Shutterstock/Neil Roy Johnson, 88, 89, 93 (bottom right); Shutterstock/Nicola Gavin, 12, 13, 31 (bottom right); Shutterstock/Nikolay Tonev, 118, 119, 123 (bottom right); Shutterstock/pix2go, 10, 11, 31 (bottom left); Shutterstock/saied shahin kiya, 74, 75, 92 (top left); Shutterstock/Sergey Popov V, 48, 49, 62 (bottom left); Shutterstock/Sportsphotographer.eu, 20, 21, 32 (bottom right); Shutterstock/Stephen Coburn, 106, 107, 122 (top right); Shutterstock/Tomo Jesenicnik 14, 15, 32 (top left); Shutterstock/TTphoto 108, 109, 122 (bottom left)

The publisher does not endorse products whose logos may appear on objects in images in this book.